EFFECTIVE
LEARNING

Alan Mumford

INSTITUTE OF PERSONNEL AND DEVELOPMENT

Design and typesetting by Paperweight
Printed in Great Britain by
Short Run Press, Exeter

British Library Cataloguing in Publication Data
A catalogue record for this book is available from the
British Library

ISBN
0-85292-617-0 (pack of five)

**INSTITUTE OF PERSONNEL
AND DEVELOPMENT**

IPD House, Camp Road, London SW19 4UX
Tel.: 0181 971 9000   Fax: 0181 263 3333
Registered office as above. Registered Charity No. 1038333.
A company limited by guarantee. Registered in England No. 2931892.

EFFECTIVE LEARNING

Alan Mumford

Alan Mumford has worked in such firms as John Laing & Sons, IPC Magazines, International Computers Ltd, and the Chloride Group. He was also deputy chief training adviser at the Department of Employment. In 1983 he was appointed professor of management development at International Management Centres, and is still visiting professor there. He has worked with senior managers and directors and developers in a variety of organisations, including Ford of Europe, Pilkington, Brooke Bond, and Unison. He has published numerous articles and books, including *Management Development: Strategies for action*, published by the IPD.

TRAINING EXTRAS is a comprehensive series covering all the crucial management skill areas. Each booklet includes the key issues, helpful starting points and practical advice in a concise and lively style. Together, they form an accessible library reflecting current best practice – ideal for study or quick reference.

Other titles in the series include:

The Appraisal Discussion Terry Gillen

Asking Questions Ian MacKay

Businesslike Budgeting Eric Parsloe and Raymond Wright

Customer Care Frances and Roland Bee

Listening Skills Ian MacKay

The Manager as Coach and Mentor Eric Parsloe

Managing Your Time Iain Maitland

Motivating People Iain Maitland

Negotiating, Persuading and Influencing Alan Fowler

The Selection Interview Penny Hackett

Working in Teams Alison Hardingham

The Institute of Personnel and Development is the leading publisher of books and reports for personnel and training professionals and students and for all those concerned with the effective management and development of people at work. For full details of all our titles please telephone the Publishing Department on 0181 263 3387.

 # Contents

Chapter 1   **Introducing Effective Learning**   1

Chapter 2   **The Learning Process**   4

Chapter 3   **Using Learning Opportunities**   17

Chapter 4   **Developing Myself**   28

Chapter 5   **The Context for Learning**   32

Chapter 6   **People Who Help**   35

Chapter 7   **Conclusion: Effective Learning Principles**   38

Further Reading   40

1

 **Introducing Effective Learning**

Why is learning important?

After they leave school, university, or professional education people learn most of the time in an unstructured informal way. They would say they learn a great deal over their lives, without necessarily being able to identify either what they want to learn or what they have learned. When professionals and managers talk about 'learning from experience' they are rarely describing a process which has been carefully organised, properly reviewed and fully understood. This means that as managers and professionals they have not been encouraged to see learning as a *normal* managerial or professional activity – where of course they would expect to organise and review their work.

Yet as our working worlds change around us, the need to learn efficiently, effectively, and quickly grows. What we learned to do well five years ago, especially in areas affected by technology, may no longer be available or appropriate. The relatively secure lifetime careers that at least some people enjoyed are less likely to be available. Even with one employer, the content of the job may have significantly changed – think of management in hospitals, de-layering in many organisations, or changes in views about the 'customer'.

Managers and professionals need to acquire the knowledge, skills and insights demanded in the jobs they do. But to do this effectively they need to do more than rely on vague understandings that you learn by experience (or by the occasional injection of a book or course). Nor can they rely on half-remembered, accidental, and perhaps no-longer-relevant learning. They need to be assisted to learn more effectively from a variety of experiences – and this means helping them to learn how to learn.

The benefits of learning

Most people do not learn things unless there is a purpose to the learning, especially in the work context. Different people seek different benefits including:

- a wish to increase their competence in their current work
- a wish to develop their competence in new areas of skill or knowledge
- a wish to improve their career prospects
- a wish to improve the personal satisfaction they get from their work
- a less immediate wish to gain the rewards associated with any of the above – financial, psychological, or social.

Exercise 1

1. Think about your response to the benefits listed above.

2. Score yourself on each of them, from 10 = strong reason for learning, to 0 = low reason.

3. Are there any other benefits you recognise from improving your capacity to learn?

What do we mean by learning?

Sir Winston Churchill is supposed to have said that 'I am always willing to learn, though I do not always like being taught'. This is a very important distinction which will be the basis for much of what is described in this book. Learning has at least two meanings:

- the process by which we acquire knowledge, skills, or insight
- the end result of the process – achieved knowledge, skills, or insight.

Learning is achieved through a variety of methods. Some of them, usually described as training or education, are formally structured with the aim of enabling someone to learn. (But, as Churchill implied, formal processes do not suit everyone.) Learning is also brought about by the experiences we have in and around work (and of course also in our lives away from work). This is often described as 'learning from experience'. One of the issues is that education and training are inputs, designed and controlled by educators and trainers. But they are not the same thing as learning in terms of the second definition, ie achieved learning. What someone else tries to teach you may not result in your achieved learning.

Some writers have also tried to distinguish between learning and development. This approach is associated with a view that learning can be *incremental*, which means adding to your existing knowledge, skills and insights but within the current context, or *transformational*, which means developing knowledge, skills and insights related to a changed view of what the job is all about. Although the objectives and content of learning or development, incremental or transformational learning, can be very important to particular individuals in specific circumstances, these are not issues of prime concern to most individuals most of the time. Certainly, to aim at the more difficult objectives of transformational learning without first having fully understood and worked through incremental learning experiences is unlikely to be successful.

A definition of learning

Learning has happened when people can demonstrate that they know something that they didn't know before (insights and realisations as well as facts) and/or when they can do something they couldn't do before (skills). This definition is my own, and clearly other people have other definitions. As is the case throughout this book, my definitions, descriptions, exercises, and value judgements about what is important are presented. As a practical workbook, intended to secure action by individuals, it seems more important to provide a clear message, even though it may sometimes seem egotistical, than to provide a balanced review of what a number of different authors have said; so you will not find references to left and right brain, or to the difference between cognitive and behavioural learning theory. Equally, the emphasis throughout is on managers and professionals, because that is the world in which I work, and through which I have developed the ideas presented here.

Exercise 2

1. Look back over your working life. Select two experiences from which you have learned a great deal. They may, for example, be tasks you have completed, people you have worked with, courses you have attended, books you have read.

2. Add to your review of successful, positive, helpful learning experiences two which you see as unhelpful or unsuccessful.

3. To what do you attribute the success or failure of the experiences in terms of your achieved learning?

4. If you wish, extend your review to your life outside work.

2

The Learning Process

There are five major reasons why people do not learn as effectively as is desirable:

- They do not recognise an activity as learning – they simply see it as 'doing a piece of work'.
- They partially recognise something as involving learning, but fail to use the opportunity fully.
- An off-the-job learning experience is badly designed and/or implemented.
- The opportunity for learning is provided in a way which fits poorly with the way in which an individual likes to learn.
- The learning opportunity is not perceived as relevant to the needs of, and benefits sought by, the learner.

For many years formal training and education focused on the last of these as the prime reason why people did not learn, so the discussion focused on the desirability of analysing needs carefully and of generating motivation and commitment in the learner. Certainly this point is absolutely desirable when it comes to formally designed learning experiences – an instruction book, a course, or a video should be provided with content which is both well delivered and appropriate to the needs of the particular learner.

Since, however, most of us, most of the time, learn through activities not primarily designed as learning experiences, but through the normal work we do, there is a growing recognition that we need to focus much more on *how* we learn rather than exclusively on whether we want to learn. We now have a way of describing the learning process which is both readily understandable and usable by any of us. In its most straightforward version, it takes the view that since we learn mostly by doing things and then thinking about how we have done them, the learning sequence can be set out as shown in Figure 1.

The initial focus given here to learning from an activity – from an experience – presents a logical sequence as shown in the cycle, often starting with the experience itself (of course, you may have planned the

Figure 1

THE LEARNING CYCLE

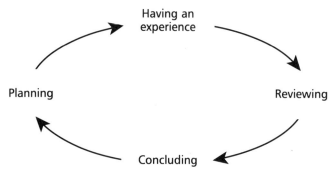

Honey & Mumford, *The Manual of Learning Styles* (see p. 40).

experience in which case you will have started at that stage of the learning cycle, but that is a relatively rare initial step).

Readers may immediately recognise the validity of the cycle from two points of view. The first is that the cycle presents a sequence recognisable to most of us, although we may not have thought about it before. A second point is that while most of us follow the 'experience to plan' sequence through our normal work, many courses are designed differently. They often present someone else's conclusions – and then ask you to review and reflect on them. For some learning requirements this may be the right sequence, but this design is probably overused – another possible explanation for the Churchill aphorism given earlier.

On the face of it the answer should be that all designed learning experiences should take people round the cycle in appropriate balance and sequence, and that all activities at work which contain learning potential should similarly be analysed and monitored through each stage of the cycle.

Exercise 3

1. Does your view of how you and others learn coincide with the learning cycle?
2. Can you think of an experience where you have gone round the cycle 'in appropriate balance'?
3. Can you think of an experience where you have not gone round the learning cycle 'in appropriate balance', and now feel that you could have learned more if you had done so?
4. Can you think of a recent, current or near-future activity to which you could apply the learning cycle in order to generate more learning for yourself (eg more time on reviewing, more opportunity to develop and test conclusions)?

Preferred ways of learning

If everyone followed the learning cycle by giving sufficient attention at each stage of the cycle then we would increase the chance of learning effectively. Indeed individuals and groups with whom I have worked have been able to adopt the learning cycle as a way of improving their learning. They often tell me there is nothing remarkable about it – 'after all, it is just the way we ought to be thinking through our managerial/professional work'.

Figure 2

THE TASK CYCLE

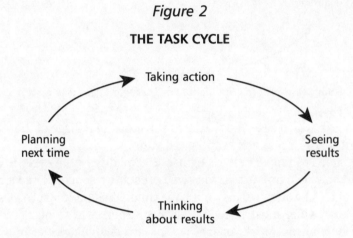

Honey & Mumford, *The Manual of Learning Styles* (see p. 40).

However, the fact is that not all structured learning experiences are designed in a balanced way, nor do all on-the-job experiences seem to lend themselves obviously to the application of the discipline of the cycle.

In addition, effective learning for individuals requires a recognition that one of the reasons why individuals do not learn fully from any particular experience is that it may not match the way in which they like to learn. Individuals have likes and dislikes about how they learn just as they may prefer opera to ballet, westerns to mysteries, sunning on a beach to trekking around mountains. So we have no reason to be surprised by the fact that different people have different reactions to an apparently similar experience which could involve learning. Away from work, some will regard a charismatic performance to 500 people by an American guru as a significant learning experience, while others will come away complaining that there is nothing of specific and practical value to their organisation. Some people are excited by the improved understanding of leadership gained by leading a group of managers in an outdoor or adventure training task, while others will complain there was not sufficient time to think about what was going on. At work, some people will sit down carefully and plan what they will learn from a new project, will ensure for themselves time to review what has happened and try to apply lessons learned. Others faced with the same kind of experience will be impatient about the time suggested for planning and reviewing, and simply want to get on with the job.

Like many trainers, my colleague Peter Honey and I had for many years recognised that individuals differed in their willingness or ability to learn from particular learning experiences, even though they initially seemed committed and motivated to do so. We discovered the innovative work of David Kolb which provided the explanation in a more usable form than simply that of 'some people learn differently from others'. His version of the learning cycle, and his 'learning styles inventory', stimulated us to develop our own view on the learning cycle, and our own learning styles questionnaire.

Figure 3

THE LEARNING CYCLE AND STYLES

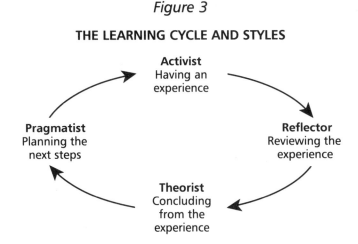

Honey & Mumford, *The Manual of Learning Styles* (see p. 40).

The full details of our approach are available in the resources described at the end of this book. Our learning styles questionnaire is accompanied by a set of general descriptions of four learning styles. Scores resulting from the completed questionnaires indicate whether or not an individual has a strong preference to learn through one, or perhaps more, of the learning styles. Strong scores indicate the likelihood of a good match, low scores indicate that an individual is less likely to learn in that particular way. The styles are consistent with the four stages of the learning cycle – so one of the reasons why individuals do not give appropriate attention to each stage of the cycle is that they simply do not like that particular kind of learning. Some managers are very good at throwing themselves into activities and generating a lot of experience, but are much less effective at reviewing what they have learned from the experience. Some managers are very interested in general ideas and concepts, whereas others are much less inclined to be attracted to what they probably call theory, and are more interested in practical ideas and techniques.

The learning styles material goes on from the scores and the general descriptions to indicate more specific activities from which individuals with these styles are likely to learn.

The following are abbreviated versions of preferred ways of learning for the four styles.

Activists. Learn best from relatively short here-and-now tasks. These may be managerial activities on the job or on courses: such things as business games and competitive team-work exercises. They learn less well from situations involving a passive role such as listening to lectures or reading.

Reflectors. Learn best from activities where they are able to stand back, listen, and observe. They like collecting information and being given the opportunity to think about it. They learn less well when they are rushed into things without the opportunity to plan.

Theorists. Learn best when they can review things in terms of a system, a concept, a model or a theory. They are interested in and absorb ideas even where they may be distant from current reality. They learn less well from activities presented without this kind of explicit or implicit design.

Pragmatists. Learn best when there is an obvious link between the subject matter and the problem or opportunity on the job. They like being exposed to techniques or processes which can be applied in their immediate circumstances. They learn less well from learning events which seem distant from their own reality. 'Does it apply in my situation?'

Here are some examples of individuals with strong preferences from a group with whom I worked. (Individuals with low preferences would express the opposite view about the likelihood of learning.)

Strong activist Mr White welcomes the additions to his job and is not disturbed by the uncertainties involved. He enjoys taking on the new tasks and responsibilities. He is sure he will pick up some new ideas, but does not think you can plan that sort of thing.

Strong reflector. Ms Brown says the collection of data has always been fundamental to her approach to her job. The need she expresses to assess the effectiveness of her relationships with her colleagues could be met in part by encouraging her to make notes after significant meetings.

Strong theorist. Mrs Green has attended two management courses at different business schools. She says she enjoyed the diversity of experience among faculty and other participants. She rated some of the faculty very highly in terms of intellectual quality.

Strong pragmatist. Mr Red says he left a course on managing time half-way through because he saw no way of being able to apply it in the reality of his job.

Of course much the most accurate and therefore valid way of assessing whether you have strong preferences about how you learn is to do the learning styles questionnaire – see Further Reading. However, it could be useful at this stage for you to test your immediate reaction to the idea of learning style preferences, and perhaps to your own possible position.

Exercise 4

1. Is it your experience that there are significant differences in the way in which some individuals learn?

2. Do you have an immediate reaction of agreement that one or more of the styles statements is strongly true about you – or most unlike you?

3. Look back at your two most helpful and two least helpful learning experiences; might there be a relation to any strong, or any low, learning style preferences?

4. Can you think of a colleague with whom you have had an experience which suggests that he or she has a strong learning style preference?

5. What conclusions do you draw from your answers to the first three questions?

6. Which stages of the learning cycle have you gone through in reading these statements about the learning cycle and learning styles?

Dealing with preferences

You may have noticed that in the preceding sections a significant part of the learning cycle was not fully covered – planning the next steps.

One potential plan was implicit in the statements about the learning cycle – that it is both possible and desirable to apply the learning cycle as a discipline to any learning experience offered to you – whether a course, a task, a new job, or working with new colleagues.

Exercise 5

1. In addition to your answer to Exercise 3 how might you incorporate the idea of the learning cycle into your ongoing work? Can you pick out particular activities or something of special significance?

2. Is there someone with whom you can share the reviewing and concluding aspects?

Learning style results tell us only what we are now in terms of preferred ways of learning; they are not fixed forever. They are sometimes affected by the particular context in which an individual works – which might encourage more or less reflection, for example. Even more positively, it is possible for some people to attempt deliberately to change their moderate or low learning style preferences by changing the behaviours that have caused that result.

Exercise 6

1. Do you have sufficient information about your learning style preferences to discuss with someone else your likely response to particular kinds of learning opportunity (eg your manager, training or personnel officer)?

2. Does it seem that there are some kinds of activity from which at the moment you will find it difficult to learn? Can you find some other way of meeting whatever need was intended to be met by such an activity?

3. Can you attempt to build up your potential as a learner by expanding your learning style preferences? To whom can you talk about this?

More on how we learn

The idea of the learning cycle and learning styles advanced first by Kolb and then by Honey and myself has been shown to have practical application by thousands of managers and professional people over the last 20 years. But it ought not to be the last word, and is certainly not the only word that can be said about learning.

The other most significant discovery about learning was associated with its originator Professor Reg Revans – *action learning*. This elevates the common sense observation, that we learn a great deal by doing things, into a more rigorously argued case for structuring learning through real work, via a defined significant problem or project, and with the help of other people facing similar problems. He argues that while there is a case for imparting knowledge to others (he has, after all, written several books and scores of articles on action learning), people often learn more, and more effectively, from work on real problems. He defined the difference between P (programmed knowledge, available through books, experts, etc), and Q (questioning about problems, not led by experts and not having pre-ordained solutions).

Revans, together with Kolb, had the most powerful influence on my own understanding of, and work in, learning. His basic premise and framework offers potential for combining real work and learning at a level of significance and powerful impact on an organisation; powerful (and some would say risky) precisely because of the association of work of real significance with learning from that work. The action learning process places a learning structure around a significant experience. However, the difference from what managers often talk about in terms of learning from experience is that action learning emphasises the processes, disciplines and interactions involved in squeezing every possible element of learning out of a major experience. Revans as a scientist produced an equation about learning:

$$P \text{ (programmed knowledge)} + Q \text{ (questioning)} = L \text{ (learning)}$$

I have had what some would regard as the temerity of adjusting his equation to:

$$Q + P + Q = L$$

My case for doing this is that I want to avoid the implication that programmed knowledge always comes before the questioning. I propose the reverse – that individuals have to ask intelligent questions before knowing what programmed knowledge might be appropriate. The programmed knowledge may then generate ideas for additional questioning.

The questions posed before deciding what P is required vary according to the people involved, but will often in my case include:

- What are your main objectives?
- What do you have to do well in order to meet these objectives?
- What are the significant obstacles which may prevent you doing things well?

The answers to these questions give clues to what problems/opportunities should be worked on, eg:

- What is the difference between being a director and being a manager?
- We need to diversify our range of products/services.

Also the questions and problem statements tell you what P might be relevant, eg:

- written material and discussion of what those involved actually do
- tutorials on strategy.

The significance of Revans in the context of the arguments so far in this book is that action learning provides the bridge between learning from significant, but often accidental, experiences in and around the job, and learning experiences designed off the job specifically for learning. While many management educators and trainers profess a belief in the desirability of doing 'real work' on courses, the action learning process provides a stronger philosophical and practical integration between real work and designed learning. Given the view adopted here that effective learning is learning that is implemented rather than simply knowledge acquired, action learning (when properly designed and applied fully in principle) can be a most powerful tool.

Attempts to differentiate between different kinds of learning, and the attribution of the word 'development' to some, are not necessarily helpful, as has been argued earlier. More relevant to most learners is the question 'are not different kinds of learning process appropriate to different kinds of learning requirement?' As an example, the most efficient way of learning how to use a word processor is probably not simply to acquire a word processor and experience playing with the keys – a manual accompanied by a skilled instructor is likely to be better! Work done by Sylvia Downs and Patricia Perry has provided a simple form of differentiation which can be very helpful in identifying exactly how it is that you propose to learn:

Learning by memorising. This enables individuals to recall material in the same form as it was originally learned.

Learning by understanding. Understanding is an active mental process involving thoughts which link or group ideas in a new way that makes sense to the individual.

Learning by doing. This involves learning a procedure and then practising it until the individual becomes skilful.

This threefold analysis has the acronym MUD. It is perhaps in some senses a different way of looking at the learning cycle, since it contains three of the four stages of the cycle.

Collective differences

There could be a middle position between 'all people learn or should learn in the same way', and 'it is impossible to generalise about how individuals learn'. Do identified groups tend to learn well in one way and less well in another? Specifically, are there differences in how, for example, women learn as compared with men, or how different nationalities learn?

The research on how women's learning style preferences compare with men's is contradictory. On David Kolb's learning styles inventory there are significant differences between men and women, but on the Honey and Mumford learning styles questionnaire there are not. There may be issues about whether women choose to, or are forced to, behave in learning terms in the same way as men, as it is often argued that they are required to do in other aspects of their managerial and professional lives. It is clearly the case that whatever the argument about learning style preferences, women are often still disadvantaged in terms of the provision of learning opportunities, the context in which they take them up, and the behaviour of men towards them both at work and in any specific learning environment.

Information available from the learning styles questionnaire suggests that there are some significant national differences in responses. While, for example, managers and professionals from the United States, Australia and the United Kingdom are very close in their total response, other nationalities have different responses.

In relation to both women and nationality issues, however, the preponderant concern for readers of this book is really the individual assessment 'what am I like as a learner?', rather than 'how do I compare with other learners?'

The skills of learning

The theme of this book is the close association between real work and learning. The significance is in part that we do not therefore require individuals suddenly to operate differently in their work role and in their learning role – indeed the fact that some people have attempted such a differentiation explains some of the lack of success of some efforts to teach people skills or knowledge.

My research and reading of others' research shows me that there are no skills which are uniquely and solely learning skills. Rather there are some skills which effective managers and professionals would expect to have which can usefully be highlighted as particularly applicable in pursuit of learning. My priority list is:

- questioning
- listening
- reviewing
- sharing
- observing
- relating a to b (conceptualising)
- accepting help
- monitoring.

Exercise 7

1. Score yourself on a scale from 0 = not very good, to 10 = very good on each of these skills in relation to *learning*. (Note the emphasis – you might have to decide that you are better at these in your work role than you are in your learning role.)

2. If there are some low scores, how important do you perceive them to be in terms of your effectiveness as a learner?

3. What could you do to improve the skills? (See Further Reading, *The Opportunist Learner*.)

These skills, as already indicated, are general skills which can be focused on for learning. In addition there are some specific actions you could undertake (each of which could, of course, embrace a number of different skills):

Effective learning behaviour

1.   Set standards of performance for yourself in your job.

2.   Review your achievements against those standards.

3.   Identify what areas you need to learn (knowledge, skill or insight) in order to perform more effectively.

4.   Identify the available opportunities for learning (see later in this book).

5.   Analyse what in your work environment will help or hinder you in learning.

6.   Consider the likely impact of any preferred learning styles, and any strengths or weaknesses in learning skills.

7.   Draw up a personal learning/development plan.

Exercise 8

Review each of these behaviours. Have you recently attempted each of these? What do your answers to earlier exercises now add?

Group learning skills

A great strength of action learning is that it emphasises the issue of learning with and from other people. Since it is relatively recently that serious work has been done on individual learners, perhaps it is not surprising that little has been done to emphasise the skills of learning from and with other people in a group. The comments in Figure 4 (on page 16) about learning-groups are drawn from the general experience of myself and others, rather than from data-based analysis through research or questionnaires.

All groups in which you work are potentially vehicles for learning for yourself and others. You may not have thought about the groups or teams to which you belong in those terms, so it may be unlikely that you have thought about your own behaviour in such groups in terms of facilitating learning by yourself and others. Exercise 9 on page 16 enables you to do that.

Figure 4

INDIVIDUAL BEHAVIOURS IN EFFECTIVE LEARNING GROUPS

Enabling fellows to share air time appropriately

Non-defensive about own actions and learning

Supportive about issues/concerns of others

Open in initiating and responding to issues

Analytical

Questioning in style, eliciting information – not defensiveness

Listening effectively

Accepting help

Creative in response to problems

Innovative in recognising learning from task

Risk-taking

Use task and learning cycle

Understand and use learning styles

Use strengths of others as learners

Help motivate others as learners

Exercise 9

1. Review yourself on a scale from 0 = not very good, to 10 = I am good at each of the behaviours in Figure 4.

2. Consider another member of the group whom you think may be an effective learner. Which of their behaviours illustrate to you that possibility?

3. What might you do to improve any low scores you have?

4. With whom could you share your analysis, conclusions and suggested actions?

3

Using Learning Opportunities

In this section we shall be looking at:

- activities specifically designed for learning – eg courses, reading, videos, books
- activities primarily created as tasks, but containing learning potential, eg conducting an interview, participating in meetings, solving a problem, planning an activity.

So far in this book emphasis has been centred particularly on learning through the second type of opportunity. This chapter looks first at specially created learning, but not because it is more important or has more priority. Rather it is because when experiences have been especially identified, designed, or created in order to provide learning for you, it is even more important that you do not miss opportunities to learn from such activities.

Some of the requirements for effective learning from courses, etc have already been identified:

- The activity ought to relate to learning/development needs which you recognise and are committed to.
- The learning process ought to give appropriate emphasis to all stages of the learning cycle.
- If there is a substantial emphasis on one stage of the cycle, that emphasis ought to be congruent with your own preferred learning style.

These issues can be brought together in a personal development plan, the features of which will be discussed in the next chapter.

The fact is that quite a lot of off-the-job opportunities for learning are not identified through an initial careful analysis of needs, through an appraisal, or personal development plan. The opportunity may have arisen through an in-company catalogue of courses, a brochure from a training centre or business school, or a leaflet from a conference organiser. In addition to the general points made earlier about the conditions that need to exist before any course is likely to be an effective choice, there are of course steps which could be taken to check factors such as:

- competence of tutors
- track record of the organisers and of the particular course
- references from previous attendees
- specific relevance to your organisation (in addition to its relevance to your general needs)
- cost/duration/location.

For most learners, once the crucial issue of the relevance of any programme to individual needs has been assessed, the next most important issue is integration of the programme into the real work situation. This means, particularly, ensuring that the reason for attendance on the programme has not only been discussed with the immediate manager, but that commitment to the individual's objectives in attending the programme, and to discussing the results afterwards, has also been obtained. Effective learning never takes place when participants say simply 'I've been sent' and are not able to identify real commitment or objectives either from themselves or from their managers. (See Mumford, *How Managers Can Develop Managers*, [Further Reading] for more detailed information on this.)

Given that learners none the less often appear on courses without the ideal of pre-discussions and commitment, there are still steps that any learner can take to gain full benefit. The following exercise will help.

Exercise 10

1. How might you best share your experiences with others on the course? (Perhaps in a more considered way than simply a chat in the bar!)

2. Think about what is being offered on the course and how you are reacting to it. In what ways could you get more value from the course?

3. What useful contacts for future use can you establish on this course?

4. What insights can you share afterwards with colleagues at work?

5. What opportunities are there on this course for risk-free experiments with relationships and skills? How could you capitalise further?

6. How might you test your own past experiences against what is offered in the course?

(This exercise is taken from *The Opportunist Learner* by Peter Honey and Alan Mumford, 2nd edn, 1995.)

Learning opportunities at work

The good news is that everything you do at work is potentially a learning opportunity. The bad news is that opportunities are often not recognised and not used, or if recognised are not used as fully as they could be. A prime reason for this, as indicated earlier, is a failure to recognise and use the discipline of the learning cycle.

The following list focuses on managerial and professional work:

Figure 5

FORMAL OPPORTUNITIES

	Column 1 I am using this for learning now	Column 2 I could use this in future
Being coached		
Being counselled		
Having a mentor		
Job rotation		
Secondments		
Stretched boundaries		
Special projects		
Committees		
Task groups		
External activities		
Internal courses		
External courses		
Reading		

Exercise 11

Tick those items in Column 1 which you are currently using as part of a formal conscious development plan.

Tick in Column 2 items which, now you think about them, you could pursue/ask for in the future.

Figure 6

INFORMAL LEARNING OPPORTUNITIES

The following list reviews more informal learning opportunities, ie those not identified in advance through a plan or scheme, but which none the less you might be able to use.

Analysing mistakes

Attending conferences or seminars

Being coached or counselled

Being mentored

Budgeting

Championing and/or managing changes

Covering for holidays

Dealings with colleagues and peers

Dealings with subordinates

Dealings with your boss

Domestic life

Familiar tasks

Giving a presentation

Interviewing

Job change in a new function

Job change within same function

Job rotation

Making decisions

Meetings

Negotiating

Networking

Performance appraisals

Planning

Project work

Reading

Same job with additional responsibilities

Secondments

Solving problems

Unfamiliar tasks/work

Working in groups/teams

Working with consultants

What else? Note additional learning opportunities below.

(This list is taken from *The Opportunist Learner* by Peter Honey and Alan Mumford, 2nd edn, 1995.)

Exercise 12

1. Go through the items in Figure 6, and place a score on the range from 0 = not at all, to 10 = strongly, on how far you believe you are using these consciously as learning opportunities at present. Be tough with yourself – you will not achieve anything by giving yourself high, but unrealistic scores. After all, no one else sees your scores.

2. Select one or two of your low scores, and consider how you might in future be able to take advantage of them as learning opportunities.

3. Who might help you in squeezing learning out of these opportunities?

Four approaches to learning from experience at work

The learning cycle and its associated learning styles model is an effective way of looking at how individuals learn from any kind of experience. Given the focus most people have on learning from experience, it can additionally be valuable to look at another model. This arose from a research project which looked at what actually precipitated learning, and how the learning was achieved. This revealed essentially four different approaches:

- intuitive
- incidental
- retrospective
- prospective.

As with the learning cycle and learning styles, the desirable situation would be that all learners consistently used a combination of retrospective and prospective approaches. Many management development schemes are based implicitly on the assumption that managers can be encouraged to plan their development (prospectively), and can be encouraged to think (retrospectively) about their learning. The learning cycle model emphasises the same point. The fact is, however, that a lot of people are not willing or able to use all four approaches, and for some of them a leap into total retrospective or prospective approaches is not practicable. As with learning styles, therefore, the more sensible idea is to enable people better to understand their current approach to learning from work experiences, and then to enable them to take a step rather than a leap. The following exercise facilitates this:

Read through the following descriptions and then answer the questions that follow (Exercise 13).

The intuitive approach. The intuitive approach involves learning from experience, but not through a conscious process. The person using the intuitive approach claims that learning is an inevitable consequence of having experiences. If questioned, he or she is able to talk in detail about a variety of different experiences, describing what happened and what was achieved. The learning or developmental aspects are rarely, if ever, referred to. Indeed, the intuitive approach sees managing and good business practices as synonymous with learning. Someone using the intuitive approach, therefore, finds it difficult and unnecessary to articulate what they learned or how they learned it. They are content that learning occurs through some natural process of osmosis.

Typical quotes from users of this approach are:

'I'm sure I'm learning all the time but I can't be more specific.'

'I just do it but I can't tell you how.'

'I do that already without calling it learning.'

'I suspect you are doing it all the time without realising you're doing so.'

Since people using the intuitive approach put their trust in learning as a 'natural', effortless process, they find it difficult to accept that there are advantages to be gained by making the process more deliberate and conscious, either for themselves or for other people.

The incidental approach. The incidental approach involves learning by chance from activities that jolt an individual into conducting a 'post-mortem'. A variety of things can act as jolts but common ones are when something out of the ordinary crops up or where something hasn't gone according to plan. Mishaps and frustrations often provide the spur.

When something hits people using the incidental approach they are inclined to mull over what happened in an informal, unstructured way. They may do this in odd moments such as while travelling between appointments or home from work or 'in the bath'. People using incidental learning tend to use the benefit of hindsight as a way of rationalising, even justifying, what happened. As a result, they may jot something down 'for the record' but not in the form of learning points, more as an insurance in case, subsequently, they need to cover themselves.

Typical quotes from users of this approach are:

'I learn from the unfamiliar parts of my job, not from the bits I am already familiar with and have already mastered.'

'If you know how to do something, you aren't going to learn from it.'

'It's the originality of the experience that provokes more reflection.'

'You *only* learn from your mistakes.'

People using the incidental approach often find it easier to conduct their post-mortems by talking things over with someone else, preferably someone who was also present during the experience in question.

The retrospective approach. The retrospective approach involves learning from experience by looking back over what happened and reaching conclusions about it. In common with the incidental approach, the retrospective approach is especially provoked by mishaps and mistakes. In addition, however, people using this approach are more inclined to draw lessons from routine events and successes. They therefore extract learning from a diverse range of small and large, positive and negative, experiences.

People using the retrospective approach conduct reviews, sometimes in their heads, sometimes in conversation and sometimes on paper. The sequence, slowed down, looks like this:

The outcome in the retrospective approach is that considered conclusions are knowingly reached. An individual by reviewing, acquires knowledge, skills and insights or has them confirmed and reinforced. Skills-based courses often provide opportunities for conscious retrospective learning – though opportunities are not always used properly.

Typical quotes from users of this approach are:

'It helps to hold things up to the light.'

'Reviewing is essential to put things into perspective.'

'You never really understand something until you write it down.'

The prospective approach. The prospective approach involves all the retrospective elements but includes an additional dimension. Whereas retrospection concentrates on reviewing what happened *after* an experience, the prospective approach includes planning to learn *before* an experience. Future events are seen not merely as things to be done which are important in their own right, but also as opportunities to learn. Individuals using this approach are expectant learners with their antennae constantly tuned in to the possibility of learning from a whole variety of experiences.

In the event, what the individual *expected* to learn may not in fact materialise quite as planned. But the process of thinking about learning in advance makes it likely that they will extract *some* learning from the situation, rather than drawing a blank.

The sequence in prospective learning is:

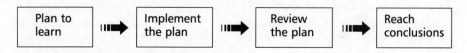

Again, courses provide clear opportunities for this approach – but there are often weaknesses in implementation.

Typical quotes from users of this approach are:

'I learn because I go there expecting to do so.'

'There is no substitute for thorough planning, not only to get things done but also to learn from doing them.'

'Sorting out what you want to get in advance increases your chances of getting something worthwhile.'

Having read the descriptions of four different approaches to learning, review your own approach through Exercise 13 opposite.

Examples of how to improve your approach

Moving from intuitive to incidental. The incidental approach is one you will tend to want to use more often with more exciting, non routine, perhaps particularly difficult experiences.

EXAMPLE

I gave a presentation at an important management meeting three weeks ago. It went over very badly – I didn't get agreement to the things I wanted, some of my colleagues wouldn't look me in the eye afterwards and I heard on the grapevine that the MD wasn't pleased. I can't put my finger on what went wrong or why, but I'll do it differently next time.

This is a typical intuitive example – the manager knows that something went wrong, so he has learned, but he is not sure why it went wrong.

Exercise 13

1. Which approach do you use

Most often?	Least often?

2. In what circumstances do you tend to use the different approaches? Complete each of the following sentences:

I am inclined to use the intuitive approach when…

I am inclined to use the incidental approach when…

I am inclined to use the retrospective approach when…

I am inclined to use the prospective approach when…

If your analysis tends to show that you more often use the intuitive and incidental approaches, plan how you could increase your use of the retrospective and prospective approaches:

From *The Opportunist Learner* by Peter Honey and Alan Mumford, 2nd edn, 1995.

It is also characteristic, however, of a potential incidental approach – because clearly it was a jolt to his self confidence! Moving from intuitive to incidental here would involve the manager concerned in pinpointing why things went wrong instead of simply accepting that they did. Without this he or she will probably make changes in his or her presentation next time without necessarily putting right the things which were crucially wrong. At its simplest, he or she needs more data, for example from colleagues and the MD.

Moving from incidental to retrospective. The first illustration shows how more thought can convert from intuitive to incidental in the context of a rather stressful experience. If, however, individuals learn only from their most stressful experiences, they will miss some potentially important experiences. The basis of this approach is to consider all kinds of activities as potential learning experiences, not just the most stressful. The important word here is *consider*. You will not be able to review and act on *all* your activities.

EXAMPLE

A sales manager had been involved in a particularly difficult negotiation with a customer. For some years she had been used to dealing with the same person, and she was suddenly faced with someone different with a very aggressive style of behaviour. Travelling home in the car afterwards she thought about how she had handled the negotiation and what she would do differently next time. So she had set about learning from this new experience.

To add a retrospective approach to what is essentially an incidental approach, she needed to extend this particular experience to other experiences. Was her experience in dealing with this particular sales manager really unique? Should she review other experiences of handling customers with whom she had not dealt before? Or alternatively, could she, in looking back, find that she had a general problem in dealing with aggressive people?

Moving from retrospective to prospective. The shift required between these two approaches is potentially both the most productive and yet the most difficult. It is potentially productive because like any other form of planning, looking ahead increases the chance that you will achieve something successfully. It is the most difficult because some of the most exciting and interesting learning experiences cannot be identified in advance, and sometimes things that you think will happen don't happen.

EXAMPLE

> A marketing manager had recently been involved in a task-force set up
> to manage the introduction of a new product. The task-force had existed
> for nine months, and involved representatives from all major functions
> in his company. Halfway through the period of the task-force a director
> who used to be his boss casually asked him what he was learning from
> it. It struck him at that time that his answer was not very full. So he
> started to keep a note of some of the more interesting things he had
> learned. By accident, towards the end of the project he met the director
> again, and this time was able to tell him much more about what he had
> learned.

This is highly characteristic of a thoughtful manager actually generating improved understanding of his learning through the retrospective approach. One step for further improvement he decided for himself – in future he would keep up his weekly learning log. However, that was simply a useful discipline for the retrospective approach. To convert to a prospective approach he needed to think about the next stages of the project and try to identify in advance what sort of experiences might occur, and what he might learn from them. Also, he could apply this process to future similar action. There would be new experiences, new colleagues, different objectives, different stresses. He might choose to adopt a different style of working. All these represent additional learning opportunities which could be identified through the prospective approach.

Complementarity or alternatives?

The analysis available to the learner through the four approaches is desirably to be seen as complementary to the learning cycle and learning styles model, something which enables people to look more closely at a particular aspect especially related to learning at work. Learners will gain most from the overall review of all kinds of learning experience offered through the learning cycle and learning styles. They will, however, gain additional benefit from the specific focus of the four approaches, directed as it is at those opportunities which arise most frequently – at work.

4

Developing Myself

Although a great deal of emphasis has been given so far to taking advantage of accidental and informal opportunities, learning effectiveness will be enhanced by an appropriate plan. Chapter 2 described the essentials of 'effective learning behaviour', which provide the basis for a personal development plan.

Exercise 14

Revisit Exercise 8 – effective learning behaviour. Also look at the answers you have provided to Exercises 11 and 12 on learning opportunities. What would you now add in order to create a personal development plan?

Using feedback from others

The analysis of your development needs so far has concentrated on your own perceptions. It would also benefit you to think about how other people see your performance and your development needs.

Exercise 15

1. Review all the information you have been given on your performance in your job through a formal process such as appraisal or performance review.

2. What information and ideas have been generated from this in identifying development needs?

3. What information do you have on any development you may require for other tasks or jobs in your organisation?

Although important, these formal processes do not always work in a timely or effective fashion. Most of us receive feedback from others, not through an organised meeting or discussion or form-filling, but from people who have volunteered observations on our performance, or from whom we have requested feedback.

Exercise 16

1. What major tasks, projects or other significant items of work have you completed recently on which you may have received feedback from your manager, colleagues, subordinates or clients?

2. What was the feedback?

3. What did it indicate about your development needs?

Now put together your responses to the last two exercises and consider what additional elements, if any, you would now add to your personal development plan.

It will be noted that there are two options in terms of how your personal development plan is created. The first exercise in this sequence enabled you to focus, through opportunities, on development possibilities. The second option took a more traditional management development route of working from carefully identified needs. These are options which could be shown to be complementary, not single choice alternatives.

Personal development plans – another approach

Some people may be able to participate in an extended version of the personal development plan process illustrated above, perhaps creating a personal development plan as a specific objective, rather than through adding together different elements, as illustrated earlier. I use the following list of topics for this purpose:

1. managerial experience to date
2. own perception of current job requirements, skills, knowledge, competences
3. own view on career plans
4. own perception of development needs
5. own perception of strengths

6. own perception of areas for improvement
7. development experiences to date
8. development opportunities
9. current work providing opportunities
10. current created work opportunities
11. courses
12. other suggestions.

Items 9 to 12 are the suggested responses or 'development solutions'. These will take account not only of needs but also of learning style preferences.

The final element needed is a statement of what action will be taken, by whom on the proposed 'development solutions', and when the PDP will be reviewed.

Continuing professional development

It is easy to say that learning needs to be a lifelong process. At one level it is in the sense that most of us do continue to learn throughout at least our working lives – though we do not necessarily do so efficiently and effectively. The personal development plan approach outlined above is a process which should be revisited at least once a year, and preferably also in association with any major job change or change in the working environment.

The Institute of Personnel and Development provides serious encouragement for its members to engage in lifelong learning through its continuing professional development policy and supporting documents (see Further Reading).

Recording learning

For CPD purposes, and for the processes encouraged through the Management Charter Initiative, a record of learning is a requirement. However anyone interested in enhancing learning should keep a learning log or diary in some form. The essentials of the learning log take you round the learning cycle, and the following simple format can be included in your diary or filofax if you do not wish to keep a separate document:

- my description of what happened
- my conclusions/lessons learned
- my plan to do something better/different.

Although strong reflectors have the most natural attraction to this process, theorists like it because it enables them to 'draw things together', and pragmatists like it because it enables them to focus particularly on things to do differently. Activists are less inclined to use a learning log – they find it difficult or 'I don't need to write it down'. They need extra support from colleagues or from learning groups in order to undertake this!

5

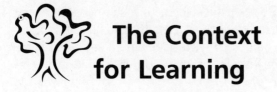 **The Context for Learning**

The models and exercises used so far show how much more individuals can do for themselves. However, there is a range of influences on a learner, as shown in Figure 7:

Figure 7

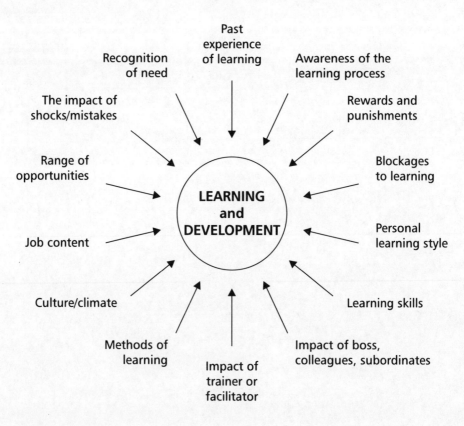

Exercise 17

1. On a scale from 0 = not at all, to 10 = very powerful, assess the impact on you of each of the influences in Figure 7.

2. Select one of the low score items and consider what action you might take to make the influence more positive.

3. What help might you seek and from whom?

The environment for learning

All learning depends on actions by individuals. Some of those actions, however, are taken with other people – with your manager, with colleagues in a group, with the organisation as a whole. Effective learning has to be built through each of these, and sensibly by taking each step as shown in Figure 8, the learning pyramid.

Figure 8

THE LEARNING PYRAMID

Increasing attention now is being paid to the idea of the learning organisation, which is shown as the peak of the pyramid. My definition of the learning organisation is:

> creating an environment where the behaviours and practices involved
> in continuous development are actively encouraged.

The emphasis here is on behaviours and practices specific to learning. (Some writers on the learning organisation embrace such a wide variety of useful management behaviours that the emphasis on learning is lost.) For the individual learner, the question is how far the work environment encourages learning. There are some detailed questionnaires available to enable you to assess this (see Pearn and Mulrooney; Pedler, Burgoyne and Boydell; and Honey and Mumford in Further Reading). A much simplified version which will give an idea of the issues involved is the following:

Figure 9

THE LEARNING CULTURE

- Encourages managers to identify their own learning needs.
- Provides a regular review of performance and learning for the individual.
- Encourages managers to set challenging learning goals for themselves.
- Provides feedback at the time on both performance and achieved learning.
- Reviews the performance of managers in helping to develop others.
- Assists managers to see learning opportunities on the job.
- Seeks to provide new experiences from which managers can learn.
- Provides or facilitates the use of training on the job.
- Tolerates some mistakes, provided managers try to learn from them.
- Encourages managers to review, conclude, and plan learning activities.
- Encourages managers to challenge the traditional ways of doing things.

Exercise 18

1. Review each of the factors listed above for your unit/division/organisation as a whole.
2. Mark on a scale from 0 = low, to 10 = high, the extent to which you believe the criteria to be currently met.
3. Which of these has the most powerful effect on your own learning?
4. What action might you take to try to improve some of the low scores?
5. What help would you like, and from whom, to achieve this?

6

 People Who Help

A number of the exercises so far have included a question on who might help individuals learn more effectively. The following figure shows the range of people who might be available.

Figure 10

POTENTIAL HELPERS IN DEVELOPMENT

On the Job	Off the Job
• Boss	• Tutors/Trainers/Facilitators
• Grandboss	• Consultants
• Colleagues	• Friends
• Subordinates	• Partner
• Mentors	• Participants on educational or training programmes
• Clients	• Participants in professional activities
• Professional advisers – internal	• Participants in voluntary activities
• Professional advisers – external	
• Management development committee	

(Updated version of Figure in *Management Development: Strategies for action* – see Further Reading)

As we move away from a focus on solo work on learning opportunities, we can recognise not only the range of potential helpers, but also an important issue about help when it is directed at improved learning. It is not necessarily a one-way process, in which someone else helps you. Not only might you have a helping relationship in the sense indicated in Figure 10 with someone else; you may be helped by someone else who also learns from the experience. So the experience can be one of reciprocal learning – though the participants may, of course, learn quite different things.

Exercise 19

1. Consider the list of potential helpers in Figure 10.

2. Have any of these individuals given you any help in learning from an experience?

3. Has the help been explicitly understood by either of you as being about learning?

4. Or has the help really been 'to understand or do my job better' with a subsequent awareness of what you learned? Were you aware at the time, or very soon afterwards, that you had learned something?

5. What skills or behaviours did the helper display which helped you to learn?

6. What did you learn that may help you to help others (either learning about the process of helping, or about the content of whatever help you received)?

Exercise 20

- Revisit your personal development plan, Figure 10 and Exercise 19 on helpers.

- Would you now add to your ideas on who might help you on the development opportunities identified in your personal development plan?

Creating a learning environment

A positive environment in which individuals learn is influenced by a number of factors (see Figure 7) and, as we have just seen, by a number of different individuals who may help. The most powerful influence is likely to be your manager. The manager has four roles which support and encourage your learning:

Figure 11

MANAGING A LEARNING ENVIRONMENT

- *Role model*
  You need to be a role model by explicitly demonstrating in your behaviour and actions that you are an enthusiastic learner/developer yourself.

- *Provider*
  You need to be a conscious and generous provider of learning/development opportunities for other people and an active supporter/encourager whenever those opportunities are taken up.

- *Systems*
  You need to build learning into the system so that it is integrated with normal work processes and is firmly on the conscious agenda.

- *Champion*
  You need to champion the importance of learning for other parts of the organisation and the organisation as a whole.

(From *Managing Your Learning Environment*, Peter Honey and Alan Mumford, 1995)

Exercise 21

1. If you are a manager, assess yourself on a scale from 0 = low, to 10 = high, on how well you do on each of these roles.

2. Review your direct manager, and score on the same scale.

3. What can you do:
   - to improve your own score?
   - to influence your manager's score?

7

Conclusion: Effective Learning Principles

Effective learning involves the following principles:

- It is a sequential total process.
- It involves skills and behaviours which can be developed – you are not born with or without the ability to learn effectively.
- It builds on experience.
- For most managers and professionals most of the time learning is centred around work.
- For most managers and professionals (not just pragmatists) learning is embraced more enthusiastically when it is specific and implementable rather than hypothetical and abstract.
- It is primarily driven by the individual's motivation, needs and interests.
- Learning is individual in the sense of differences of need and of preferred ways of learning.
- Learning is social in the sense of opportunities, situations (eg groups), and feedback.
- Although the learning cycle and learning styles are powerful influences on individuals, there is sometimes a 'best method' of learning a particular skill or knowledge.
- People learn from difficulties and problems, but need to review the causes of successes as well.
- Learning is never finished; it is life long.

Figure 12

LEARNING AS A CONTINUOUS PROCESS

 # Further Reading

Learning processes

CHRIS ARGYRIS, *Reasoning, Learning and Action*, San Francisco, Jossey-Bass, 1982.

CHRIS ARGYRIS, 'Teaching Smart People to Learn', *Harvard Business Review*, May/June 1991.

SYLVIA DOWNS, *Learning at Work*, London, Kogan Page, 1995.

PETER HONEY and ALAN MUMFORD, *The Manual of Learning Styles*, Third Edition, Honey, 1992.

PETER HONEY and ALAN MUMFORD, *Using Your Learning Styles*, Second Edition, Honey, 1995.

MALCOLM KNOWLES, *Andragogy in Action*, San Francisco, Jossey-Bass, 1985.

DAVID KOLB, *Experiential Learning*, Hemel Hempstead, Prentice Hall, 1983.

MIKE PEDLER (Editor), *Action Learning in Practice*, Second Edition, Aldershot, Gower, 1991.

REG REVANS, *Action Learning*, Blond and Briggs, 1980.

Learning opportunities

PETER HONEY and ALAN MUMFORD, *The Manual of Learning Opportunities*, Honey 1989.

PETER HONEY and ALAN MUMFORD, *The Opportunist Learner*, Second Edition, Honey, 1995.

MIKE McCALL, MIKE LOMBARDO and ANGELA MORRISON, *The Lessons of Experience*, Lexington Books, 1988.

Developing myself

CHARLOTTE CHAMBERS, JOHN COOPE and ADRIAN McLEAN, *Develop Your Management Potential*, London, Kogan Page, 1990.

INSTITUTE OF PERSONNEL AND DEVELOPMENT, *Continuing Professional*

Development Pack, London, IPD, 1995. (Available to IPD members only.)

MIKE PEDLER, JOHN BURGOYNE and TOM BOYDELL, *Managers Guide to Self Development*, Third Edition, Maidenhead, McGraw Hill (UK), 1994.

The learning context

PETER HONEY and ALAN MUMFORD, *Managing Your Learning Environment*, Honey, 1995.

ANDREW MAYO and ELIZABETH LANK, *The Power of Learning*, London, IPD, 1994.

ALAN MUMFORD, *How Managers Can Develop Managers*, Aldershot, Gower, 1993.

ALAN MUMFORD, *Learning at the Top*, Maidenhead, McGraw Hill (UK), 1995.

ALAN MUMFORD, *Management Development: Strategies for action*, Second Edition, London, IPM, 1993.

MICHAEL PEARN and CHRIS MULROONEY, *Tools for a Learning Organisation*, Second Edition, London, IPD, 1995.

MIKE PEDLER, JOHN BURGOYNE and TOM BOYDELL, *The Learning Company*, Maidenhead, McGraw Hill (UK), 1991.

PETER SENGE, *The Fifth Discipline*, New York, Doubleday, 1990.

KAREN WATKINS and VICTORIA MARSICK, *Sculpting the Learning Organization*, San Francisco, Jossey-Bass, 1993.